Far East Chinese for Youth

远东少年中文

(Simplified Character)

Character Book
Level 2

Wei-ling Wu   吴威玲

Hai-lan Tsai   蔡海澜

Jean Yu   俞建军

远东图书公司

The Far East Book Co., Ltd.

Published by

The Far East Book Co., Ltd.

66-1 Chungking South Road, Section 1

Taipei, Taiwan

www.fareast.com.tw

Distributed by

US International Publishing Inc.

39 West 38th Street

New York, New York 10018

U.S.A.

www.usipusa.com

ISBN 957-612-573-1

A few words from the authors

Character Book–Level Two is designed to help you to learn to read and write in Chinese characters more efficiently. Here are some important features about the format of this book that you should know:

The first page of each lesson contains single characters and character combinations that are required for this lesson. This page is meant to give you a clear idea of the stroke order and meaning for the characters. There will be reinforcement drills in the following pages.

The second page of each lesson provides you with character combinations that connect the new characters and learned characters. They are arranged in groups for you to learn as connected chains and to compare for discovering differences.

You will become familiar with these character combinations by writing the pinyin or the English meaning for each group of combinations.

The third page of each lesson allows you: 1) to apply new characters in a reading situation; 2) to learn how to figure out the meaning of an unknown character through the context; and 3) to practice how to get information in spite of unknown characters.

While reading the passage on this page, please focus on making meaning. If you come across an unknown character that is underlined, be sure to read the characters around it and take a guess of its meaning. Then keep on reading and check your understanding. At the end of this page, there are some bonus questions for those who are willing to take a risk in reading.

The fourth page of each lesson brings you a step further in using the characters for reading and writing tasks. A wide range of tasks, from single sentence writing to authentic reading, reinforce your reading and writing skills and, most importantly, connecting the basic skill learning with the real world.

Contents

Lesson One

1 地 dì　　earth, ground	**2** 图 tú　　picture	**3** 方 fāng　square; direction	**4** 边 biān　directional suffix
5 城 chéng　　city	**6** 过 guò　suffix for verbs	**7** 长 cháng　　long	**8** 第 dì　ordinal prefix

dì						
earth						
地						
地						
地						
地						
地						

9		10	
从	来	亚	洲
cónglái	all the time	Yàzhōu	Asia
11		12	
世	界	首	都
shìjiè	world	shǒudū	the capital of a country

Character Combinations:

地方	dìfang	place
地图		
中国地图		
世界地图		
一张地图		

第一		
第二		

北京		
南京		
东京		

亚洲		
美洲		

东北		
东南		
东西		
东边		
东方		
东京		

我家		
国家		

城市		
长城		
中国城		

人口		

Differentiate Characters:

弟弟	dìdi	
第一	dì yī	

首都	shǒudū	
…都是…	… dōushì …	

Reading and Writing Tasks:

I. Read the following paragraph and answer the questions **in English**:

上海在中国的东方。上海是中国第一大城，世界第三大城。上海有很多人口。上海人说上海话，也会说北京话。上海有很多商店。很多人喜欢去上海买东西。上海还有一个地方，叫老城隍庙。那儿好玩极了，又有吃的又有玩的。

1. In what part of China is Shanghai?

2. Is Shanghai the biggest city in China?

3. Is Shanghai the biggest city in the world?

4. What dialects can Shanghai people speak?

5. Why do people like to go to Shanghai?

Bonus questions for intelligent guesses:

1. What is 老城隍庙? What is special about it?

2. What does it mean by 好玩极了?

II. Finish the chart below using the example shown in the first row:

Some new words in the chart:

面积(miànjī area)   平方公里(píngfāng gōnglǐ square kilometer)

比较(bǐjiào compare)

洲名 （中文）	洲名 （英文）	面积 （万平方公里）	面积比较 （中文）
亚洲	Asia	4,400	(the biggest) 最大
非洲		3,029	(the 2nd)
北美洲		2,422	(the 3rd)
南美洲		1,800	(the 4th)
南极洲		1,400	(the 5th)
欧洲		1,000	(the 6th)
大洋洲		897	(the smallest)

III. Write the following sentences **in characters** according to the pinyin given:

1. Shìjièshang yǒu qī dà zhōu.

2. Yàzhōu shì shìjiè dì yī dà zhōu.

3. Yàzhōu bǐ Nánměizhōu dà de duō.

4. Nánměizhōu bǐ Běiměizhōu xiǎo.

Lesson Two

13 店 diàn store	14 银 yín silver	15 送 sòng send	16 给 gěi give
17 到 dào to	18 次 cì M.W. for verbs	19 影 yǐng shadow	20 院 yuàn yard

21		22	
食 品		公 司	
shípǐn	food	gōngsī	company
23		24	
银 行		一 起	
yínháng	bank	yìqǐ	together

Character Combinations:

饭店		
书店		
鞋店		
花店		

到中国		
到中国去		
到美国来		

两次		
几次		
很多次		
好多次		

电话		
电影院		

公司		
老公公		

买东西		
卖东西		

食品公司		
图书公司		

一双鞋子		
一双筷子		

这儿		
那儿		
哪儿		

Differentiate Characters:

鞋子	xiézi	
写字	xiězì	

远	yuǎn	
院	yuàn	

Reading and Writing Tasks:

I. Read the following paragraph and answer the questions **in English**:

下个星期三是我爸爸的生日。我要送给爸爸什么礼物呢？爸爸去过中国两次，所以他很喜欢中国的小东西。离我们学校不远的地方有一个中国食品公司，那儿卖食品，也卖很多小东西。我可以去那儿给爸爸买一双筷子，还买一张「生日快乐」的中文生日卡。

1. When is the author's father's birthday?

2. How many times has the author's father been to China?

3. What kind of things does the author's father like?

4. Is the Chinese food market far from the author's school?

5. What does the author want to buy for his father?

Bonus questions for intelligent guesses:

1. What does 礼物 mean?

2. What is a 生日卡?

II. Read the following sentences and answer the questions **in characters**:

1. 这儿有两家食品公司。

   What stores are here? _____.

2. 银行离我家很远。

   What is far away from my home? _____.

3. 我常常和我的朋友一起去看电影。

   What do I often do with my friend? _____.

4. 昨天妈妈送给我一双中国鞋子。

   What gift did my mom give me yesterday? _____.

III. Match the places in the left column with the activities in the right column by drawing lines.

饭馆	看电影
电影院	看书
超级市场	喝茶
银行	买礼物
花市	吃饭
茶馆	卖花
书店	卖食品
礼品店	存钱 (cún qián–to deposit money)

Lesson Three

25 前	26 后	27 左	28 右
qián　　front	hòu　　behind	zuǒ　　left	yòu　　right
29 路	30 街	31 走	32 再
lù　　road	jiē　street, avenue	zǒu　　walk	zài　　again

33 门	34 开	35 怎	36 向
mén door	kāi open; drive	zěn how	xiàng toward

37 中间	38 工作
zhōngjiān middle	gōngzuò work

Character Combinations:

前边		
后边		
右边		
左边		

北京西路		
南京东路		
中山北路		

在路口		
在学校		
在家		
在…工作		
在写字		

这么		
什么		
怎么走		
怎么去		
怎么说		
怎么写		
怎么开		

开车		
开门		
向前开		

走到学校		
走到书店		

Differentiate Characters:

在	zài	
再	zài	

工作	gōngzuò	
公司	gōngsī	

Reading and Writing Tasks:

I. Read the following paragraph and answer the questions **in English**:

马文：

　　你出校门，坐95路车，在中山北路下车，向前走，在第二个路口向右转，就是北京大街，再向前走一点儿，在路的右边有一个书店，我家就在书店的前边，北京大街23号。

小林

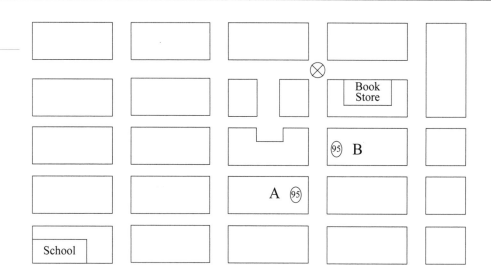

1. Where does 马文 live? Mark the map with a star.

2. Where is 北京大街? Where is 中山北路? Mark them on the map.

3. Which bus stop will 小林 get off at, A or B?

Bonus questions for intelligent guesses:

1. What is 95路车?

2. What does it mean by 向右转?

II. Match the questions on the left with the appropriate answers on the right by writing the letter in the parentheses.

( ) 1. 你爸爸在哪儿工作？　　　　A. 不远，就在电影院的后边。

( ) 2. 你每天怎么去上学？　　　　B. 向前走。

( ) 3. 你家离电影院远吗？　　　　C. 不是，她在写字。

( ) 4. 请问，银行怎么走？　　　　D. 我坐校车去上学。

( ) 5. 她在看书吗？　　　　　　　E. 他在食品公司工作。

III. Write characters according to the pinyin given:

1. Qǐng wèn, qù yínháng zěnme zǒu?

2. Zài dì èr ge lùkǒu xiàng zuǒ zhuǎn.

									转		

3. Wǒ bàba měitiān kāi chē qù gōngsī gōngzuò.

4. Xiān kàn shū, zài qù wán.

IV. Arrange the following characters according to their radicals:

街　叫　什　作　行
右　你　吃　得　件
后　很　向　他　问

街	行			
作				
向				

Lesson Four

39 班 bān　　　class	40 里 lǐ　　　inside	41 外 wài　　　outside	42 信 xìn　　　letter
43 封 fēng　M.W. for letters	44 住 zhù　　　live	45 常 cháng　　　often	46 闹 nào　　　noisy

47

觉得

juéde   feel

48

已经

yǐjīng   already

49

而且

érqiě   in addition

50

地址

dìzhǐ   address

Character Combinations:

中文班		
上班		
下班		

十多年		
很多年		

国外		
外国		
外文		
外国语		

地址		
地名		
地方		

外边		
里边		

一封信		
看信		
写信		
写信给		

城里		
城外		

所以		
可以		

Differentiate Characters:

所以	suǒyǐ	
已经	yǐjīng	

觉得	juéde	
我得去	wǒ děi qù	

Reading and Writing Tasks:

I. Read the following letter written by Xiaoming and answer the questions **in English**:

哥哥：

　　我来美国已经十多天了，去了旧金山、纽约，也去了几个中、小城市。我觉得美国的小城市很美，街上有很多树，家家门前也都有花，而且在<u>上下班的时间</u>，街上也不太闹。要是我能在这儿<u>多住几天</u>，那有多好啊！可是明天我得到<u>南美洲</u>去。

小明

1. How long has Xiaoming been in America?

2. Where has he been ?

3. Does Xiaoming like small cities in America? Why?

4. Does he have to leave?

5. What will he do tomorrow?

Bonus questions for intelligent guesses:

1. What do you think <u>上下班的时间</u> refers to?

2. What does <u>多住几天</u> mean?

3. Where is <u>南美洲</u> ?

II. Choose the phrases that best express the meaning given in English:

1. You want to ask directions to the movie theater.

   a) 请问，去电影院怎么走？
   b) 请问，电影院叫什么名字？
   c) 请问，我要去电影院，行不行？

2. You want to ask Xiao Lin where he works.

   a) 小林，你有没有工作？
   b) 小林，你在什么地方工作？
   c) 小林，你是做什么工作的？

3. You ask whether Xiao Li lives in the city or outside of the city.

   a) 小李住在城里还是城外？
   b) 小李住在城里什么地方？
   c) 小李住在里边还是外边？

4. You would like your friend to write to you often.

   a) 请你每天写信给我，好吗？
   b) 请你给我写一封信，好吗？
   c) 请你常常给我写信，好吗？

III. Write the opposite for each combination following the example given:

里边	外边	上班	
(inside)	(outside)	( )	( )
前边		左边	
( )	( )	( )	( )
城外		下边	
( )	( )	( )	( )
后门		买东西	
( )	( )	( )	( )

Lesson Five

51 桌 zhuō　　　desk	52 椅 yǐ　　　chair	53 床 chuáng　　　bed	54 园 yuán　　　garden
55 客 kè　　　guest	56 房 fáng　　　room	57 楼 lóu　　　building	58 室 shì　　　room

59	60	61	
洗	手	厕	所
xǐ　　　　wash	shǒu　　　hand	cèsuǒ　　　　　　　　bathroom	
62	63		
虽	然	不	但
suīrán　　　　　　　though	búdàn　　　　　　　not only		

Character Combinations:

中间		
房间		
洗手间		

楼上		
楼下		
地下		
地上		

房子		
房间		
书房		
车房		

方桌子		
长桌子		

花园		
菜园		

前门		
后门		
大门		
校门		

左手		
右手		
洗手		

男厕所		
女厕所		

Differentiate Characters:

方	fāng	
房	fáng	

先	xiān	
洗	xǐ	

Reading and Writing Tasks:

I. Read the following ad from a Chinese department store and answer the questions **in English**:

中国光大百货商场

楼上：<u>家具</u>（中式桌子、椅子、床、柜）

日用百货、床上用品、厕所用品

楼下：<u>家用电器</u>、服装、礼品、食品

营业时间：上午九时---晚上十时

地　　址：北京东城区西大街325号

电　　话：(10)6504-3637

传　　真：(10)6504-3641

1. Where is the bed and bath section?

2. Where is the food section?

3. Is the store open at 7:00 am?

4. On which avenue is the store located?

5. Where is this store, in Beijing, Nanjing, or Shanghai?

Bonus questions for intelligent guesses:

1. In the above advertisement, 家具 includes 桌子, 椅子, 床, etc.
   Can you figure out the meaning of 家具？

2. What does it mean by 家用电器？

II. Circle the proper character combinations for the following sentences:

1. 书桌在（洗手间　书房　厕所）里。

2. 汽车在（书房　电影院　车房）里。

3. 房子（上面　里边　前边）有草地。

4. 我家（而且　虽然　所以）小，可是很好看。

5. 大城市里（可是　所以　不但）人多，而且很闹。

6. 我不想买房子，（而且　虽然　不但）我也没钱。

III. Answer the following questions **in characters** according to the real situation:

1. 你家的房子大不大？　　　　　　＿＿＿＿＿＿

2. 你家有车房吗？　　　　　　　　＿＿＿＿＿＿

3. 你家的后边有花园吗？　　　　　＿＿＿＿＿＿

4. 你的房间在楼上还是在楼下？　　＿＿＿＿＿＿

5. 你的床是不是在房间的中间？　　＿＿＿＿＿＿

6. 你用左手还是右手写字？　　　　＿＿＿＿＿＿

7 你喜欢坐在地上看书吗？　　　　＿＿＿＿＿＿

Lesson Six

64 冰 bīng · ice	65 等 děng · wait	66 就 jiù · then, right after	67 厅 tīng · hall
68 卧 wò · lie down	69 浴 yù · bath	70 见 jiàn · see	71 草 cǎo · grass

72 时候 shíhou time, moment

73 知道 zhīdao know

74 或者 huòzhě or

75 告诉 gàosu tell

Character Combinations:

好吃		
好喝		
好玩		
好看		

回来		
回去		
回家		
回信		
回学校		

20室		
卧室		
浴室		
地下室		

看见		
再见		
明天见		

客厅		
饭厅		

喝茶		
喝冰水		

什么地方		
什么时候		

马上		
地上		

Differentiate Characters:

茶	chá	
菜	cài	

回来	huílai	
会来	huìlái	

Reading and Writing Tasks:

I. Read the following paragraph and answer the questions **in characters**:

我家的房子前边有一个小花园，花园里有红花绿草，很好看。楼上有三个卧室，爸爸妈妈的卧室里有浴室。我的房间虽然比爸爸妈妈的卧室小，可是有很多好玩的东西。还有一个卧室是客房，客人来了就住在这个房间里。楼下是客厅和饭厅，还有妈妈做饭的厨房。

1. What is in front of the house?

2. Where are the bedrooms?

3. What is in the parents' bedroom?

4. What does the author think of his room?

5. What rooms are downstairs?

Bonus questions for intelligent guesses:

1. What do you think 客房 is used for? What is 客人?

2. What is a 厨房?

II. Answer the following questions **in characters** according to the real situation:

1. 你的卧室里有什么？ _____

2. 你的书桌在什么地方？ _____

3. 你家的客厅里有电话吗？ _____

4. 饭厅里有什么？ _____

5. 冰水在什么地方？ _____

III. Read the ad and answer the questions:

新房子出售

四房一厅三浴

两车房，地下室

一年新，好学校

请电：908-543-0932

或者：908-543-4246

1. How many bedrooms are there in this house?

2. Is there a basement?

3. How long ago was the house built?

4. Which number should the buyer call?

IV. Write the following sentences **in characters** according to the pinyin given:

1. Wǒ bù zhīdao tā shénme shíhou huílai.

2. Tā méi gàosu wǒ tā qù nǎr.

3. Nǐ kěyǐ mǎshàng qù huòzhě míngtiān qù.

Lesson Seven

76 雨 yǔ · rain	77 雪 xuě · snow	78 云 yún · cloud	79 雷 léi · thunder
80 热 rè · hot	81 冷 lěng · cold	82 晴 qíng · fine	83 阴 yīn · cloudy; *yin*

84 笑 xiào smile, laugh	85 别 bié don't	86 样 yàng appearance; kind	87 气 qì air; energy of life
88 阳 yáng sun; *yang*	89 出 chū go/come out	90 怕 pà be afraid	91 更 gèng even more

Character Combinations:

下雨		
下雨天		
下雪		
下大雪		

太太		
太阳		
太好了		

多云		
少云		

怕冷		
怕热		

天气		
晴天		
阴天		

好玩		
开玩笑		

阴有雨		
晴时多云		

别出去		
别出来		
别笑他		
别开玩笑		

Differentiate Characters:

小	xiǎo	
笑	xiào	

比	bǐ	
北	běi	

Reading and Writing Tasks:

I. The following chart is based on the information provided in the Chinese Children's Encyclopedia by Zejian Education Press, China (1990).
Read the information and answer the questions **in English**:

世界气候之最

最热的地方	西澳大利亚的温得姆 1946年中333天的气温是32℃
最冷的地方	南极洲的冷极， 最冷的天是零下60℃
最干燥的地方	智利的一个地方， 1970年前后，有四百年没有下雨
最多雨的地方	美国夏威夷的一座山上， 每年有350天是下雨天
白天最长的地方	撒哈拉沙漠东部， 每年97%的时间有太阳
白天最短的地方	北极有186天看不见太阳

What information have you read about ... ?

The hottest place ---

The coldest place ---

The driest place ---

The place that has the most rain ---

The place that has the least sunshine ---

Bonus questions for intelligent guesses:

1. What do you think 1970年前后 refers to?

2. What does 干燥 mean?

II. Choose the question or sentence that best expresses the meaning given in English:

1. You want to ask about today's weather.

    a) 今天怎么样？
    b) 今天天气怎么样？
    c) 怎么样的天气很好？

2. You are at home. You don't want to go out, because it's a snowy day.

    a) 我不想出去，因为今天下大雪。
    b) 我不想出来，因为今天下大雪。
    c) 我不想出去，因为今天下大雨。

3. You want to say that today is much hotter than yesterday.

    a) 今天没有昨天热。
    b) 今天和昨天一样热。
    c) 今天比昨天更热。

4. No matter what the weather is like tomorrow, I will go out and have fun.

    a) 要是明天天气好，我就出去玩。
    b) 要是明天天气好，别和他一起出去玩。
    c) 天气好或者不好，我明天都会出去玩。

III. Answer the following questions **in characters**:

1. 你怕热还是怕冷？

   _____

2. 你喜欢晴天还是阴天？

   _____

3. 你觉得下雪好玩吗？

   _____

4. 这儿常常下雨吗？

   _____

Lesson Eight

92 春 chūn spring	93 夏 xià summer	94 秋 qiū autumn	95 冬 dōng winter
96 树 shù tree	97 叶 yè leaf	98 越 yuè more	99 进 jìn enter

100 夜	101 黄	102 色	103 亮
yè night	huáng yellow	sè color	liàng bright

104 以	前	105 美	丽
yǐqián before, ...ago		měilì beautiful	

Character Combinations:

白天		
黑夜		
半夜		

月亮		
星星		
太阳		

进来		
进去		
走进去		

树叶		
茶叶		

金色		
银色		
红色		
黄色		
金黄色		
白色		
黑色		
绿色		

春天		
夏天		
秋天		
冬天		

Differentiate Characters:

进	jìn	
近	jìn	

夏	xià	
下	xià	

Reading and Writing Tasks:

I. Read the following paragraph and answer the questions **in English**:

去年九月我到中国去了，在北京第二中学学中文。北京的秋天真美丽，树叶一片片金黄。晴天的夜晚，我和我的中国朋友出去看星星，看月亮，好玩极了。北京的冬天很冷，可是不常下雪。春天到了，公园里的草地绿了，花儿红了，大家都到公园里去玩。

1. When did the author go to China?

2. Where did the author study Chinese?

3. What did the author do on a fine autumn night?

4. What was the winter like in Beijing?

5. Why did people go to the park in the spring?

Bonus questions for intelligent guesses:

1. Can you see the sun shining during 夜晚 ?

2. What does 草地 mean?

II. Write characters according to the pinyin given:

1. Xiàtiān de báitiān yuèlái yuè cháng le.

2. Yǐqián wǒ bù zhīdao, kěshì zuótiān tā gàosu wǒ le.

3. Wǒ xǐhuan hóng sè de huā.

4. Dōngtiān xiàxuě zhēn měilì.

III. Choose the right word for the following sentences and translate them into English:

1. 我家离学校很_____（进，近）。

    (English: _____)

2. 别开玩_____（笑，小）了。

    (English: _____)

3. 朋友来我家，我说：「请_____」（近，进）。

    (English: _____)

4. 我每天_____（到，道）学校去上课。

    (English: _____)

5. 早上的太阳又红又_____（辆，亮）。

    (English: _____)

Lesson Nine

106 江	107 河	108 湖	109 船
jiāng　　river	hé　　river	hú　　lake	chuán　　boat

110 念	111 读	112 公	113 风
niàn　read aloud; study	dú　　read	gōng　　public	fēng　　wind

114	115	116	
并	餐	小	时
bìng at all	cān meal	xiǎoshí hour	

117	118	
活 动	飞	机
huódòng activity	fēijī airplane	

Character Combinations:

长江		
黄河		
西湖		
东海		

坐车		
坐船		

公园		
公司		

中餐		
西餐		
餐馆		

看书		
读书		

念书		
念十年级		
念几年级		

河上		
河里		
河边		

一个小时		
半个小时		
一个半小时		

Differentiate Characters:

每	měi	
海	hǎi	

念	niàn	
年	nián	

Reading and Writing Tasks:

I. Read the following paragraph and answer the questions **in English**:

中国有四条主要的大河：长江、黄河、黑龙江和粤(Yuè)江。长江是中国的第一大河，黄河是中国的第二大河。长江因为「长」，所以叫长江。黄河因为水色「黄」，所以叫黄河。夏天，很多人喜欢到长江去游泳。

1. What is the longest river in China?

2. What is the second longest river in China?

3. Why is Changjiang called 长江?

4. Why is Huanghe named 黄河?

5. What do people do in Changjiang during summer time?

Bonus questions for intelligent guesses:

1. In the sentence 中国有四条主要的大河, what does 主要的 mean?

2. What does it mean by 水色?

II. The following chart is a comparison of the length of the four major rivers in China. Choose the correct answer for each blank according to the information given:

中国四大河流长度比较表

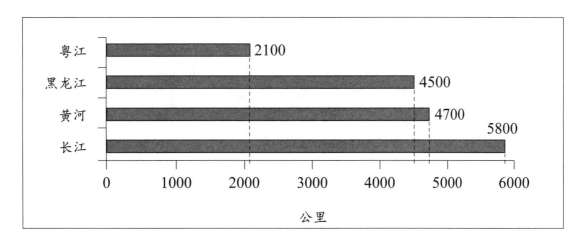

1. 长江是中国的_____大河。

    a) 第一   b) 第三

    c) 第四   d) 第二

2. 黄河长_____公里。

    a) 4500   b) 4700

    c) 5800   d) 2100

3. 黑龙江是中国的_____大河。

    a) 第二   b) 第一

    c) 第四   d) 第三

III. Translate the following sentences into Chinese characters:

1. I do not like to ride on boats at all.

2. I have a lot of activities every Sunday.

Lesson Ten

119 节	120 做	121 舞	122 把
jié　　festival M.W. for class periods	zuò　　do	wǔ　　dance	bǎ　M.W. for chairs, particle
123 拿	124 放	125 穿	126 全
ná　　pick up	fàng　　put	chuān　　wear	quán　　whole

127 忙	128 帮	129 衣	服
máng busy	bāng help	yīfu	clothes
130 恭	喜	131 这	些
gōngxǐ congratulate		zhèxie	these

Character Combinations:

初中		
初中一		
初一		
年初一		

大年夜		
年夜饭		

新年快乐		
生日快乐		
春节快乐		

过年		
过春节		
过生日		

春节		
春天		

衣服		
买衣服		
做衣服		
穿衣服		

把书拿到这儿来		
把书放在桌子上		
把书给他		
把书送给他		
把衣服穿上		

Reading and Writing Tasks:

I. Read the following paragraph and answer the questions **in English**:

去年我去中国学中文，住在中国妈妈的家里。春节到了，我们一起吃年夜饭。年初一早上我们穿上新衣服。中国妈妈给我和我的中国妹妹一人一个红包。我们还去看舞龙舞狮。我对朋友们说：「恭喜恭喜」，「新春快乐」。他们都说：「你的中文说得真好！」

1. Where did the author stay while he studied Chinese in China last year?

2. What kind of festival was it?

3. What did they do to celebrate the festival?

4. What did the author say to his friends? What did his friends say to him?

Bonus questions for intelligent guesses:

1. What is the best title for this passage?

    a) 舞龙   b) 中国在世界的东方

    c) 我学中文   d) 在中国妈妈家过春节

2. What does it mean by "中国妈妈给我和我的中国妹妹一人一个红包"？
    a) Both my Chinese sister and I each got a Red Money Bag.
    b) Only I got a Red Money Bag.
    c) Only my Chinese sister got a Red Money Bag.
    d) My Chinese sister and I shared one Red Money Bag.

II. Choose the right word for each sentence:

1. 把这些书（那，拿）到房间里去。

2. 把衣服（穿，船）上。

3. 我们（全，金）家一起吃年夜饭。

4. 请（帮，帮忙）我把书拿到车上去。

5. 他不喜欢（做，坐）飞机。

6. 我把你的笔（方，放）在桌子上了。

III. Answer the following questions **in characters**:

1. 中国年的最后一天叫什么？

2. 中国新年叫什么？

3. 中国新年的第一天叫什么？

4. 中国人过春节忙不忙？

5. 你念几年级？

6. 初中的最后一年是几年级？

Lesson Eleven

132	133	134	135
暑	寒	假	度
shǔ summer	hán winter	jià holiday	dù spend (vacation)

136		137	
学	习	打	算
xuéxí	study	dǎsuan	plan

138		139	
以 后		然 后	
yǐhòu	later	ránhòu	after, then
140		141	
希 望		应 该	
xīwàng	hope	yīnggāi	should

Character Combinations:

暑假		
寒假		
春假		
放假		
度假		

虽然		
然后		
以后		
最后		
后边		

学年		
学期		
学习		
学校		
学生		

开学		
开门		
开车		
开花		

从来不…		
从…到…		

飞机		
坐飞机		
坐飞机到		

Differentiate Characters:

以后	yǐhòu	
已经	yǐjīng	

应该	yīnggāi	
因为	yīnwèi	

Reading and Writing Tasks:

I. Read the following paragraph and then answer the questions **in English**:

今年暑假爸爸希望我能到中国去，他说我中文已经学了两年了，应该到中国去看看。我觉得爸爸的<u>建议</u>很好，在中国我不但可以学习中文，而且可以学习中国<u>文化</u>。我打算先在北京学习一个月的中文，然后坐飞机去西安，从西安坐火车去南京，再从南京坐船去上海，最后从上海飞回美国。

1. Where does the father think the author should go during the summer time?

2. Why does his father suggest that he do so?

3. What would the author do in Beijing?

4. How would the author travel from Beijing to Xi'an?

5. Where would the author go from Xi'an?   How?

6. What would be the author's last destination?

Bonus questions for intelligent guesses:

1. What does 建议 mean?

2. What is 文化?

II. Choose the question that best expresses the meaning given in English:

1. You are asking where your family should go for summer vacation.
   a) 我们全家暑假应该去哪儿度假？
   b) 我们全家什么时候去度假？
   c) 我们应该怎么去度假的地方？

2. You want to ask which bus you should take to go to the cinema.
   a) 去明星电影院，应该坐汽车吗？
   b) 去明星电影院，应该坐几路车？
   c) 去明星电影院，应该怎么走？

3. You ask your mother whether she could drive you to the post office.
   a) 妈妈，我可以开车送你去邮局吗？
   b) 妈妈，谁可以开车送我去邮局？
   c) 妈妈，你可以开车送我去邮局吗？

4. You want to find out when the new semester starts.
   a) 新学期开学多久了？
   b) 新学期什么时候开学？
   c) 新学期九月开学吗？

III. Choose the right words to make the following sentences meaningful:

1. 我在（假，家）帮妈妈做饭。

2. 我坐飞机（道，到）中国去度假。

3. 明天我们不上课，学校（度假，放假）。

4. 我先去北京，（虽然，然后）去上海。

5. 你（在，再）哪个高中上学？

Lesson Twelve

142	143	144
拍	定	礼 物
pāi　　　　　　pat	dìng　　　stable; fix	lǐwù　　　　　　gift

145	146
照 片	故 宫
zhàopiàn　　　　photo	Gùgōng　　the Forbidden City

147 本来 běnlái originally

148 后来 hòulái later

149 旅行 lǚxíng travel

150 现在 xiànzài now

Character Combinations:

本来		
本子		
日本		

照片		
一张照片		
拍照		

本来		
后来		
回来		
进来		

再见		
先…再…		
明天再去		

旅行		
旅馆		
饭馆		

一定		
一起		

过年		
过生日		

吃饭的 时候		
上课的 时候		

Differentiate Characters:

旅行	lǚxíng	
银行	yínháng	

再	zài	
在	zài	

Reading and Writing Tasks:

I. Read the following paragraph and answer the questions **in English**:

小明今年寒假到北京去旅行。回来的时候，他送给我一张他在故宫拍的照片。他还告诉我一个有意思的故事。

故宫也叫宫城，是古时候皇帝(huángdì, emperor)的家。故宫有999.5个房间，为什么要有这半个房间呢？因为天上也有一个宫城，叫天宫(the Heavenly Palace)，这个天宫有1000个房间。皇帝又叫天子，因为他觉得他是天的儿子，他的家要比天宫小一点儿，但是要比别人的家都大，所以故宫有999.5个房间。

1. Where did Xiaoming go for winter vacation?

2. How many rooms are there in the Forbidden City?

3. How many rooms did people believe 天宫 have?

4. Why does the Forbidden City have 999.5 rooms?

Bonus questions for intelligent guesses:

1. What does 故事 mean?

2. What does 儿子 mean?

II. Answer the following questions **in characters**:

1. 坐飞机的时候，你喜欢拍照吗？

_____

2. 你常常出去旅行吗？

_____

3. 你去过日本吗？

_____

4. 你住过汽车旅馆吗？

_____

5. 今年暑假你打算去哪儿度假？

_____

III. Choose the right words to make the following sentences meaningful:

1. 我明天（一定，一起）去故宫。

2. （本来，后来）我不会拍照，
（本来，后来）我学会了，觉得很好玩。

3. 去年在中国（旅行，旅馆）的时候，我们住在
（旅行，旅馆）。

4. 这是谁送给你的（旅行，礼物）？

5. 你（先在，现在）在哪个高中上学？

Lesson Thirteen

151 连 lián　　　even	152 爱 ài　　　love	153 场 chǎng　open space	154 脑 nǎo　　　brain
155 找 zhǎo　look for	156 停 tíng　　　stop	157 办 bàn　　handle	158 医 yī　cure, treat

159		160	
游泳		附近	
yóuyǒng	swim	fùjìn	nearby

161		162	
运动		重要	
yùndòng	sport	zhòngyào	important

Character Combinations:

电话				市场		
电车				菜市场		
电脑				停车场		
电影				运动场		

活动		
运动		

医生		
医院		
电影院		

教书		
教师		
教室		
卧室		
浴室		
办公室		
校长室		

校园		
花园		
公园		

常常		
经常		
已经		

饭馆		
旅馆		
图书馆		

这儿		
女儿		
儿子		

Reading and Writing Tasks:

I. Read the following paragraph and answer the questions **in English**:

王小花在第一女中学习。她的学校校园很大，有图书馆、运动场、游泳池，还有一个很美的花园。她经常和同学们在校园活动。她的教室里不但有电视机而且有电脑。学校的附近什么店都有，连电影院也有。可是王小花并不觉得她的学校是最好的。她说：「要是学校里有男同学，那有多好啊！」

1. What kinds of facilities does Wang Xiaohua's school have?

2. What does she do with her classmates?

3. Is there a movie theater in the school? Where is it?

4. Does Wang Xiaohua feel her school is the best? Why?

Bonus questions for intelligent guesses:

1. What does 第一女中 mean?

2. What does 电视机 mean?

II. Circle the facilities that your school has:

办公室　厕所　飞机场　医院　图书馆

电影院　银行　游泳池　教室　校长室

运动场　校园　停车场　公园　电脑室

医务室　食堂　食品店　旅馆　电视机

III. Choose the right words that make the following sentences meaningful:

1. （停车场，运动场，菜市场）有很多车。

2. 你的笔（找，我，早）到了吗？

3. 我早上要去看（衣，医，一）生。

4. 妹妹喜欢（有用，游泳，游水）。

5. 上课了，快进（教书，教师，教室）吧！

6. 我（经常，已经，常常）去过了。

7. （重要，要是，附近）有银行吗？

IV. Read the paragraph and answer the questions **in English**:

我在这儿住了三年了，从来没有停过电。
可是昨天晚上不但停水了，而且停电了。
我真不喜欢没有水也没有电的晚上。

1. What happened last night?

2. How did this person feel about it?

- 65 -

Lesson Fourteen

163	164	165	166
对	数	理	语
duì — correct; to	shǔ (shù math) — count	lǐ — reason, logic	yǔ — language

167	168	169
听	懂	文 化
tīng — listen	dǒng — understand	wénhuà — culture

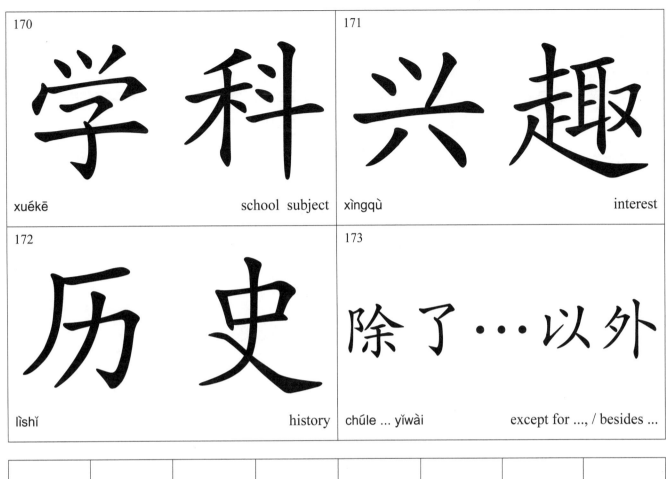

170
学科
xuékē   school subject

171
兴趣
xìngqù   interest

172
历史
lìshǐ   history

173
除了…以外
chúle ... yǐwài   except for ..., / besides ...

Character Combinations:

对不起				一些		
对不对				有些		
对中文 有兴趣				这些		
				那些		
				哪些		

英语		
国语		
外语		
语文		

高兴		
兴趣		

懂不懂		
看不懂		
听得懂		

地方		
地理		
物理		
生物		
礼物		
动物		

数学		
化学		
文化		

学科		
学习		
学期		

历史		
世界历史		
美国历史		
中国历史		

Reading and Writing Tasks:

I. Read the following paragraph and answer the questions **in English**:

马大明是一个好学生。他会说中文，英文和法文，连日文也看得懂。他的数学是全班第一。他对科学也很有兴趣。他说：「科学真好玩，我真喜欢物理和化学。」可是有一门学科他学不好。他很不喜欢历史。他说：「世界历史太长了，怎么学得会？」

1. Is Ma Daming good at foreign languages? How do you know?

2. How does he do in math?

3. What does he think about physics and chemistry?

4. What subject doesn't he like? Why?

Bonus questions for intelligent guesses:

1. What does it mean by 科学? What does it mean by 学科?

2. What is the word "门" in "一门学科"?

3. What does 学不好 mean?

II. Fill in the blanks by choosing the appropriate compounds from the ones given:

好听　好看　不懂　有兴趣　想学　喜欢

1. 中文课我越上越 _____。

2. 中国字我越写越 _____。

3. 历史我越念越 _____。

4. 生物我越学越 _____。

5. 外语我越说越 _____。

6. 法文我越听越 _____。

III. Fill in the blanks with appropriate Chinese characters:

1. 上_____课的时候，我们看地图。

2. 我___得懂中国话，但是我看不___中国字。

3. 你对什么学科最有_____？

4. 我只喜欢生物，对别的_____都没兴趣。

5. _____数学以外，我别的学科都不喜欢。

6. _____数学以外，我还喜欢生物。

7. 我想去中国学中文和中国_____。

8. 我只要这本书，_____书我都不要。

Lesson Fifteen

174	175	176	177
病	钟	才	换
bìng — be sick	zhōng — clock	cái — only (later than expected)	huàn — change

178	179	180	
饿	死	音	乐
è — hungry	sǐ — die; dead	yīnyuè — music	

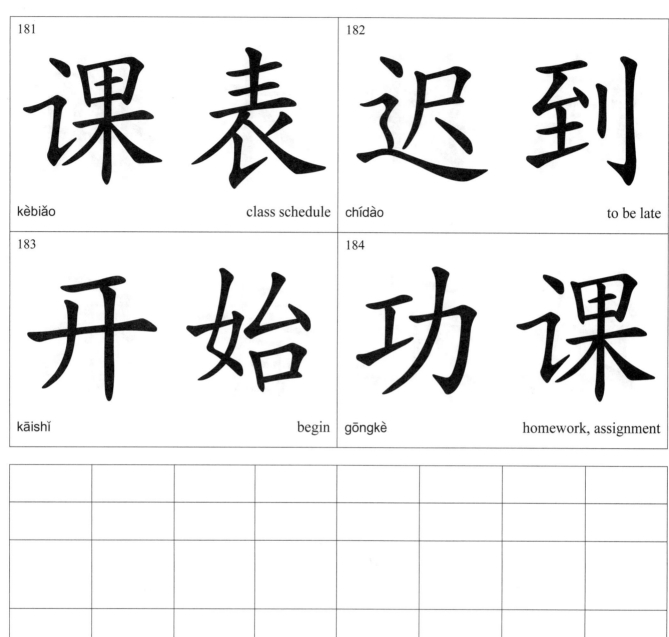

181 课表 kèbiǎo — class schedule

182 迟到 chídào — to be late

183 开始 kāishǐ — begin

184 功课 gōngkè — homework, assignment

Character Combinations:

早到		
迟到		

做功课		
上课		
下课		
课表		

一节课		
上一节课		
下一节课		

饿不饿		
饿死了		

一分钱		
一分钟		
十点钟		
几点钟		
一个钟		

开车		
开始		

生病		
看病		
病人		
她病了		

Differentiate Characters:

音乐	yīnyuè	
快乐	kuàilè	

老师	lǎoshī	
老是	lǎoshì	

Reading and Writing Tasks:

I. Read the following paragraph and answer the questions **in English**:

小李常常因为生病不能去学校上课。有一天，小李又没去上课。第二天，老师问他为什么老是生病。小李说不知道。老师又问他去看了医生没有。小李说没有。他说他从来不看医生。老师觉得很奇怪。他问小李为什么不去看医生。小李说他很怕吃药。老师对小李说：「你应该去看看医生，吃药。吃了药，你的病就会好了。」

1. Is Xiao Li often absent from school?

2. What did the teacher ask him?

3. Did he go see a doctor? Why?

4. What was the teacher's suggestion?

Bonus questions for intelligent guesses:

1. Can you figure out the meaning of 奇怪 from the context?

2. What does 吃药 mean?

II. Fill in the blanks with the characters given:

才　再　就

1. 小王今天早上十点钟___到学校。

2. 校车六点来，你最好五点钟___起床。

3. 她下午___告诉我了，我已经知道了。

4. 我饿死了，先吃饭___去看医生吧！

5. 雨越下越大了，等雨停了___回家吧。

III. Fill in the blanks with appropriate Chinese characters to make this paragraph meaningful:

　　我早上第一_____课是化学，然后上英文。我很喜欢我的课。英文课八点_____，我_____到了一分钟，老师很不高兴。我说我_____迟到了一分钟。可是老师说一分_____也不应_____迟到。吃饭的时候，虽然我_____死了，可是想到英文老师，我就吃不下了。下午还有一_____英文课，别再_____了。

Lesson Sixteen

185 完 wán finish	186 惯 guàn be used to	187 非 fēicháng 常 very
188 成 chéngjī 绩 grades, scores		189 问 wèntí 题 question, problem

190		191	
报 告		忘 记	
bàogào	report	wàngjì	forget

192		193	
考 试		句 子	
kǎoshì	examination	jùzi	sentence

Character Combinations:

成绩		
我的成绩		
考试成绩		
学习成绩		

吃不惯		
穿不惯		
住不惯		
用不惯		

吃完		
写完		
看完		
做完		

句子		
一个句子		

非常		
常常		
经常		

大考		
考试		
口试		
笔试		

问题		
问问题		
一个问题		

Differentiate Characters:

考	kǎo	
老	lǎo	

成绩	chéngjī	
城外	chéngwài	

Reading and Writing Tasks:

I. Read the following paragraph and answer the questions **in English**:

马大明要写一个有关中国文化的报告，所以星期天他去中国城买书。他一走进书店就看见林老师。他也在那儿买书。林老师说他知道有一本书很好，可是他忘记那本书的名字了。他帮马大明从上到下找了半天也没找到他要的书。后来，书店小姐帮他找到一本中文的「中国文化」。虽然马大明只看得懂一点儿，可是他觉得那本书上的照片很有用，所以他就把书买回来了。

1. Why did Ma Daming go to Chinatown?

2. Who did he see there?

3. What book did the shop assistant find for him?

4. Did Ma Daming buy that book? Why?

Bonus questions for intelligent guesses:

1. Can you figure out the meaning of 有关 from the context?

2. What does 从上到下 mean?

II. Read the sentences and answer the questions according to the information given:

1. 他怎么现在才来？学生都已经走了！

   Was he on time? Where were the students?

2. 对不起！我吃不惯中餐，也用不惯筷子。

   What do I apologize about?

3. 这个报告很长，他一天写不完。

   What is he working on? Can he finish it by the next day?

4. 我觉得成绩好的学生不一定是好学生。

   What is my opinion about students who have good grades?

5. 我看不懂这个问题，请帮帮我。

   Why do I need help?

6. 明天我们有中文和数学考试。

   What will happen tomorrow?

7. 我吃饭以前能看完这本书。

   Will I be reading this book after the meal?

Lesson Seventeen

194 箱 xiāng　box; suitcase	195 急 jí　hurry	196 还 huán　return (hái　still)	197 架 jià　shelf
198 被 bèi　by	199 借 jiè　borrow, lend	200 特别 tèbié　especially	

201 故事 gùshi story

202 古代 gǔdài ancient

203 英雄 yīngxióng hero

204 无论 wúlùn no matter

Character Combinations:

书架		
衣架		
花架		

故宫		
故事		

笑话		
说笑话		
一个笑话		
开玩笑		

借书		
借钱		
借给他了		

小说		
说话		

英雄		
英国		

古代		
现代		

特别		
别的		
别人		
别…		

Differentiate Characters:

故	gù	
古	gǔ	

还没有	hái méiyǒu	
还给你	huán gěi nǐ	

Reading and Writing Tasks:

I. Read the following paragraph and answer the questions **in English**:

王先生很爱他的儿子。无论什么，他都希望把最好的给儿子。有一天，他的儿子从图书馆借了一本古代小说回家。王先生见了说：「为什么不看新的？」他的儿子说：「都被别人借走了。」王先生就去别的图书馆找到了一本新的古代小说。他很高兴地对儿子说：「你看，爸爸把你要的新的书借来了。」他的儿子说：「我要的是<u>新写的</u>现代小说，不是新的小说。」

1. What did Mr. Wang's son get from the library?

2. What did Mr. Wang want his son to have in general?

3. What did Mr. Wang do to get what he thought his son should get?

4. Did Mr. Wang succeed in finding it? Did he succeed in pleasing his son? Why?

Bonus questions for intelligent guesses:

1. Can you figure out the meaning of <u>新写的</u> from the context?

2. What title would you give this story in Chinese?

II. Fill in the blanks by choosing the correct characters from the following:

把　给　被

1.	妹妹＿＿＿饭吃完了。
2.	书都＿＿＿借走了。
3.	我＿＿＿钱送＿＿＿那个小孩了。

III. Answer the following questions **in English**:

1. 谁是你最喜欢的美国女英雄？

2. 你最喜欢的小说书名是什么？

3. 你会不会写笑话？请写一个中文的或者英文的笑话。

4. 「我一见你就笑」是一个中文歌名。请把这个歌名翻成(fān chéng—translate into)英文。

Lesson Eighteen

205 寄 jì　　mail a letter	206 收 shōu　　receive	207 到 dào　arrive; verb suffix	208 祝 zhù　　wish
209 册 cè　　volume, book	210 剪 jiǎn　　cut	211 参加 cānjiā　　join	

212

亲 爱

qīn'ài　　　　　　　　　　dear

213

感 谢

gǎnxiè　　　　　　　　be grateful

214

愉 快

yúkuài　　　　　　　　　happy

215

航 空

hángkōng　　　　　　　aviation

Character Combinations:

航空		
航空信		
航空公司		

写信		
寄信		
一封信		
航空信		

收到		
借到		
拿到		
寄到		
放到		

谢谢		
多谢		
感谢		
谢先生		

剪纸		
信纸		
一张纸		

亲爱的		
可爱的		

祝你愉快		
祝你生日快乐		

Differentiate Characters:

因为	yīnwèi	
以为	yǐwéi	

一封信	yì fēng xìn	
一个信封	yí ge xìnfēng	

Reading and Writing Tasks:

I. Read the following letter written by Daming and answer the questions **in English**:

小王：

　　你好！新的学校怎么样？还在学中文吗？

　　我现在在学中文三。我们用的课本是《少年中文》第二册。这本课本很有意思。我们不但学中文，而且还学中国文化。我们常常参加中国文化活动。上星期我们学剪纸。我学会了剪龙。这条龙是我剪了送给你的，希望你会喜欢。

　　请常常来信。我们都很想念你。

　　　　　　祝

愉快

　　　　　　　　　　　你的老同学　大明
　　　　　　　　　　　二〇〇〇年三月十八日

1. Who is Daming writing to?

2. What does Daming learn in the Chinese class?

3. What does Daming enclose in the letter?

Bonus questions for intelligent guesses:

1. Can you figure out the meaning of 课本 from the context?

2. What does 想念 mean?

II. Fill in the blanks by choosing the correct characters from the following: (Every character in the box can be used twice.)

小　大　收信人的姓名　街道　国家　城市　门号

中文地址和英文地址不一样。

中文地址从＿＿＿到＿＿＿，先写＿＿＿，＿＿＿，

再写＿＿＿＿和＿＿＿＿，

最后才写＿＿＿＿＿＿＿＿。

英文地址先写＿＿＿＿＿＿＿＿，

再从＿＿＿到＿＿＿，写＿＿＿＿＿、＿＿＿＿＿、

＿＿＿＿＿和＿＿＿＿＿。

III. Write the following sentences **in characters** according to the pinyin given:

1. Zhù nǐ xīnnián kuàilè.

2. Nǐ de láixìn wǒ yǐjīng shōudào le.

3. Wǒ hěn xǐhuan nǐ jì gěi wǒ de shēngrì lǐwù.

4. Qǐng nǐ lái cānjiā wǒmen de xīnnián wǎnhuì.

5. Fēicháng gǎnxiè.

Character List

	Pinyin	Character	English	Character Number	Lesson
1.	ài	爱	love	152	13
2.	bǎ	把	M.W. for chairs, particle	122	10
3.	bān	班	class	39	4
4.	bàn	办	handle	157	13
5.	bāng	帮	help	127	10
6.	bàogào	报告	report	190	16
7.	bèi	被	by	198	17
8.	běnlái	本来	originally	147	12
9.	biān	边	directional suffix	4	1
10.	bié	别	don't	85	7
11.	bīng	冰	ice	64	6
12.	bìng	并	at all	114	9
13.	bìng	病	be sick	174	15
14.	búdàn	不但	not only	63	5
15.	cái	才	only（later than expected）	176	15
16.	cān	餐	meal	115	9
17.	cānjiā	参加	join	211	18
18.	cǎo	草	grass	71	6
19.	cè	册	volume, book	209	18
20.	cèsuǒ	厕所	bathroom	61	5
21.	cháng	长	long	7	1
22.	cháng	常	often	45	4
23.	chǎng	场	open space	153	13
24.	chéng	城	city	5	1
25.	chéngjī	成绩	grades, scores	188	16
26.	chídào	迟到	to be late	182	15
27.	chū	出	go/come out	89	7

	Pinyin	Character	English	Character Number	Lesson
28.	chúle ... yǐwài	除了… 以外	except for/besides...	173	14
29.	chuān	穿	wear	125	10
30.	chuán	船	boat, ship	109	9
31.	chuáng	床	bed	53	5
32.	chūn	春	spring	92	8
33.	cì	次	M.W. for verbs	18	2
34.	cónglái	从来	all the time	9	1
35.	dǎsuan	打算	plan	137	11
36.	dào	到	to	17	2
37.	dào	到	arrive, verb suffix	207	18
38.	děng	等	wait	65	6
39.	dì	地	earth, ground	1	1
40.	dì	第	ordinal prefix	8	1
41.	dìzhǐ	地址	address	50	4
42.	diàn	店	store	13	2
43.	dìng	定	stable; fix	143	12
44.	dōng	冬	winter	95	8
45.	dǒng	懂	understand	168	14
46.	dú	读	read	111	9
47.	dù	度	spend（vacation）	135	11
48.	duì	对	correct; to	163	14
49.	è	饿	hungry	178	15
50.	érqiě	而且	in addition	49	4
51.	fāng	方	square; direction	3	1
52.	fáng	房	room	56	5
53.	fàng	放	put	124	10
54.	fēicháng	非常	very	187	16

	Pinyin	Character	English	Character Number	Lesson
55.	fēijī	飞机	plane	118	9
56.	fēng	封	M.W. for letters	43	4
57.	fēng	风	wind	113	9
58.	fùjìn	附近	nearby	160	13
59.	gǎnxiè	感谢	be grateful	213	18
60.	gàosu	告诉	tell	75	6
61.	gěi	给	give	16	2
62.	gèng	更	even more	91	7
63.	gōng	公	public	112	9
64.	gōngkè	功课	homework, assignment	184	15
65.	gōngsī	公司	company	22	2
66.	gōngxǐ	恭喜	congratulate	130	10
67.	gōngzuò	工作	work	38	3
68.	gǔdài	古代	ancient	202	17
69.	Gùgōng	故宫	the Forbidden City	146	12
70.	gùshi	故事	story	201	17
71.	guàn	惯	be used to	186	16
72.	guò	过	suffix for verbs	6	1
73.	hán	寒	winter	133	11
74.	hángkōng	航空	aviation	215	18
75.	kǎoshì	考试	examination	192	16
76.	hé	河	river	107	9
77.	hòu	后	behind	26	3
78.	hòulái	后来	later	148	12
79.	hú	湖	lake	108	9
80.	huán	还	return（but: hái still）	196	17
81.	huàn	换	change	177	15
82.	huáng	黄	yellow	101	8

	Pinyin	Character	English	Character Number	Lesson
83.	huódòng	活动	activity	117	9
84.	huòzhě	或者	or	74	6
85.	jí	急	hurry	195	17
86.	jì	寄	mail a letter	205	18
87.	jià	假	holiday	134	11
88.	jià	架	shelf	197	17
89.	jiǎn	剪	cut	210	18
90.	jiàn	见	see	70	6
91.	jiāng	江	river	106	9
92.	jiē	街	street, avenue	30	3
93.	jié	节	festival	119	10
94.	jiè	借	borrow, lend	199	17
95.	jìn	进	enter	99	8
96.	jiù	就	then, right after	66	6
97.	jùzi	句子	sentence	193	16
98.	juéde	觉得	feel	47	4
99.	kāi	开	open; drive	34	3
100.	kāishǐ	开始	begin	183	15
101.	kè	客	guest	55	5
102.	kèbiǎo	课表	class schedule	181	15
103.	léi	雷	thunder	79	7
104.	lěng	冷	cold	81	7
105.	lián	连	even	151	13
106.	liàng	亮	bright	103	8
107.	lǐ	里	inside	40	4
108.	lǐ	理	reason, logic	165	14
109.	lǐwù	礼物	gift	144	12
110.	lìshǐ	历史	history	172	14

	Pinyin	Character	English	Character Number	Lesson
111.	lóu	楼	building	57	5
112.	lù	路	road	29	3
113.	lǚxíng	旅行	travel	149	12
114.	máng	忙	busy	128	10
115.	měilì	美丽	beautiful	105	8
116.	mén	门	door	33	3
117.	ná	拿	pick up	123	10
118.	nǎo	脑	brain	154	13
119.	nào	闹	noisy	46	4
120.	niàn	念	study	110	9
121.	pà	怕	be afraid	90	7
122.	pāi	拍	pat	142	12
123.	qì	气	air; energy of life	87	7
124.	qián	前	front	25	3
125.	qīn'ài	亲爱	dear	212	18
126.	qíng	晴	fine	82	7
127.	qiū	秋	autumn	94	8
128.	quán	全	whole	126	10
129.	ránhòu	然后	after, then	139	11
130.	rè	热	hot	80	7
131.	sè	色	color	102	8
132.	shíhou	时候	time	72	6
133.	shípǐn	食品	food	21	2
134.	shì	室	room	58	5
135.	shìjiè	世界	world	11	1
136.	shōu	收	receive	206	18
137.	shǒu	手	hand	60	5
138.	shǒudū	首都	the capital of a country	12	1

	Pinyin	Character	English	Character Number	Lesson
139.	shǔ	暑	summer	132	11
140.	shǔ	数	count（but: shù math）	164	14
141.	shù	树	tree	96	8
142.	sǐ	死	die; dead	179	15
143.	sòng	送	send	15	2
144.	suīrán	虽然	though	62	5
145.	tèbié	特别	especially	200	17
146.	tīng	厅	hall	67	6
147.	tīng	听	listen	167	14
148.	tíng	停	stop	156	13
149.	tú	图	picture	2	1
150.	wài	外	outside	41	4
151.	wán	完	finish	185	16
152.	wàngjì	忘记	forget	191	16
153.	wénhuà	文化	culture	169	14
154.	wèntí	问题	question, problem	189	16
155.	wò	卧	lie down	68	6
156.	wúlùn	无论	no matter	204	17
157.	wǔ	舞	dance	121	10
158.	xīwàng	希望	hope	140	11
159.	xǐ	洗	wash	59	5
160.	xià	夏	summer	93	8
161.	xiànzài	现在	now	150	12
162.	xiāng	箱	box; suitcase	194	17
163.	xiàng	向	toward	36	3
164.	xiǎoshí	小时	hour	116	9
165.	xiào	笑	smile, laugh	84	7
166.	xìn	信	letter	42	4

	Pinyin	Character	English	Character Number	Lesson
167.	xìngqù	兴趣	interest	171	14
168.	xuékē	学科	school subject	170	14
169.	xuéxí	学习	study	136	11
170.	xuě	雪	snow	77	7
171.	Yàzhōu	亚洲	Asia	10	1
172.	yáng	阳	sun; *yang*	88	7
173.	yàng	样	appearance; kind	86	7
174.	yè	叶	leaf	97	8
175.	yè	夜	night	100	8
176.	yī	医	cure, treat	158	13
177.	yīfu	衣服	clothes	129	10
178.	yǐ	椅	chair	52	5
179.	yǐhòu	以后	later	138	11
180.	yǐjīng	已经	already	48	4
181.	yǐqián	以前	before, ...ago	104	8
182.	yìqǐ	一起	together	24	2
183.	yīn	阴	cloud; *yin*	83	7
184.	yīnyuè	音乐	music	180	15
185.	yín	银	silver	14	2
186.	yínháng	银行	bank	23	2
187.	yīnggāi	应该	should	141	11
188.	yīngxióng	英雄	hero	203	17
189.	yǐng	影	shadow	19	2
190.	yóuyǒng	游泳	swim	159	13
191.	yòu	右	right	28	3
192.	yúkuài	愉快	happy	214	18
193.	yǔ	雨	rain	76	7
194.	yǔ	语	language	166	14

	Pinyin	Character	English	Character Number	Lesson
195.	yù	浴	bath	69	6
196.	yuán	园	garden	54	5
197.	yuàn	院	yard	20	2
198.	yuè	越	more	98	8
199.	yún	云	cloud	78	7
200.	yùndòng	运动	sport	161	13
201.	zài	再	again	32	3
202.	zěn	怎	how	35	3
203.	zhǎo	找	look for	155	13
204.	zhàopiàn	照片	photo	145	12
205.	zhè xie; zhèixie	这些	these	131	10
206.	zhīdao	知道	know	73	6
207.	zhōng	钟	clock	175	15
208.	zhōngjiān	中间	middle	37	3
209.	zhòngyào	重要	important	162	13
210.	zhù	住	live	44	4
211.	zhù	祝	wish	208	18
212.	zhuō	桌	desk	51	5
213.	zǒu	走	walk	31	3
214.	zuǒ	左	left	27	3
215.	zuò	做	do	120	10

Character List (by radical)

* 2/17 = Book 2 Lesson 17   (This list includes characters in Book 1 and Book 2)

	Radical	Characters								
1.	一 yī one	不 bù 1/4	一 yī 1/14	三 sān 1/14	七 qī 1/14	两 liǎng 1/18	来 lái 1/33	下 xià 1/34	上 shàng 1/34	东 dōng 1/47	亚 yà 2/1
		再 zài 2/3	而 ér 2/4	且 qiě 2/4	更 gèng 2/7	丽 lì 2/8	才 cái 2/15	事 shì 2/17			
2.	丨 gǔn through	中 zhōng 1/3	北 běi 1/47	非 fēi 2/16							
3.	丿 piě a motion, diminish	生 shēng 1/9	么 me 1/13	九 jiǔ 1/14	乐 lè 1/30	年 nián 1/31	长 cháng 2/1	舞 wǔ 2/10	重 zhòng 2/13		
4.	丶 zhǔ flame, a dot	为 wèi 1/37	亲 qīn 2/18								
5.	乙 yǐ bent	也 yě 1/5	书 shū 1/23	买 mǎi 1/46	飞 fēi 2/9	习 xí 2/11					
6.	厶 sī private	能 néng 1/27	去 qù 1/32	参 cān 2/18							
7.	人 rén person	你 nǐ 1/2	他 tā 1/4	们 men 1/4	什 shén 1/13	个 ge 1/17	会 huì 1/21	今 jīn 1/32	以 yǐ 1/39	件 jiàn 1/45	从 cóng 2/1
		作 zuò 2/3	住 zhù 2/4	信 xìn 2/4	但 dàn 2/5	候 hòu 2/6	全 quán 2/10	做 zuò 2/10	假 jià 2/11	停 tíng 2/13	化 huà 2/14
		借 jiè 2/17	代 dài 2/17								
8.	八 bā eight	八 bā 1/14	弟 dì 1/18	兴 xìng 1/33	首 shǒu 2/1	公 gōng 2/2	并 bìng 2/9				

	Radical	**Characters**									
9.	几 jī table	几 jǐ 1/17									
10.	儿 rén man	先 xiān 1/11	儿 ér 1/48								
11.	亠 tóu cover	六 liù 1/14	高 gāo 1/19	离 lí 1/48	京 jīng 1/49	亮 liàng 2/8	夜 yè 2/8				
12.	讠 yán words	谁 shéi 1/12	话 huà 1/13	请 qǐng 1/15	说 shuō 1/21	谢 xiè 1/22	课 kè 1/34	诉 sù 2/6	读 dú 2/9	该 gāi 2/11	语 yǔ 2/14
		记 jì 2/16	试 shì 2/16	论 lùn 2/17							
13.	又 yòu also	友 yǒu 1/9	又 yòu 1/31	双 shuāng 1/42							
14.	阝 yì country	都 dōu 1/7	那 nà 1/12								
15.	阝 fù mound	院 yuàn 2/2	阴 yīn 2/7	阳 yáng 2/7	附 fù 2/13	除 chú 2/14					
16.	二 èr two	二 èr 1/14	五 wǔ 1/14	云 yún 2/7	些 xiē 2/10	无 wú 2/17					
17.	厂 hǎn cliff dwelling	厕 cè 2/5	厅 tīng 2/6	历 lì 2/14							
18.	匚 fāng container	医 yī 2/13									
19.	刂 dāo knife	到 dào 2/2	前 qián 2/3	别 bié 2/7							

	Radical	**Characters**					
20.	刀 dāo knife	分 fēn 1/39	色 sè 2/8	剪 jiǎn 2/18			
21.	冖 mì cover	写 xiě 1/22					
22.	力 lì strength	动 dòng 2/9	办 bàn 2/13	功 gōng 2/15	加 jiā 2/18		
23.	十 shí ten	十 shí 1/1	真 zhēn 1/20	午 wǔ 1/40	卖 mài 1/46	南 nán 1/47	半 bàn 1/50
24.	冫 bīng ice	次 cì 2/2	冰 bīng 2/6	冷 lěng 2/7			
25.	冂 jiōng suburb	同 tóng 1/10	肉 ròu 1/42	册 cè 2/18			
26.	凵 qū utensil	画 huà 1/27	出 chū 2/7				
27.	山 shān mountain	山 shān 1/29					
28.	彡 shān hairy	影 yǐng 2/2					
29.	纟 mì silk	纸 zhǐ 1/24	级 jí 1/34	红 hóng 1/44	绿 lǜ 1/44	给 gěi 2/2	经 jīng 2/4	绩 jī 2/16
30.	彳 chì to pace	很 hěn 1/19	得 de 1/28	行 háng 2/2	街 jiē 2/3		
31.	巾 jīn napkin	师 shī 1/10	市 shì 1/46	常 cháng 2/4	帮 bāng 2/10	希 xī 2/11	

	Radical	Characters								
32.	女 nǚ female	好 hǎo 1/5	她 tā 1/5	姓 xìng 1/7	姐 jiě 1/11	妈 mā 1/16	妹 mèi 1/16	始 shǐ 2/15		
33.	口 kǒu mouth	吗 ma 1/6	哪 nǎ 1/7	叫 jiào 1/8	只 zhǐ 1/18	可 kě 1/19	唱 chàng 1/27	喜 xǐ 1/30	号 hào 1/31	只 zhī 1/36	吃 chī 1/41
		喝 hē 1/41	台 tái 1/49	品 pǐn 2/2	司 sī 2/2	后 hòu 2/3	右 yòu 2/3	向 xiàng 2/3	虽 suī 2/5	告 gào 2/6	叶 yè 2/8
		听 tīng 2/14	史 shǐ 2/14	问 wèn 2/16	句 jù 2/16	古 gǔ 2/17					
34.	囗 wéi enclosure	国 guó 1/3	四 sì 1/14	因 yīn 1/37	回 huí 1/50	图 tú 2/1	园 yuán 2/5				
35.	土 tǔ earth	坐 zuò 1/15	在 zài 1/25	块 kuài 1/38	场 chǎng 1/46	地 dì 2/1	城 chéng 2/1	址 zhǐ 2/4			
36.	艹 cǎo grass	英 yīng 1/21	花 huā 1/29	菜 cài 1/41	茶 chá 1/41	草 cǎo 2/6	黄 huáng 2/8	节 jié 2/10			
37.	工 gōng work	左 zuǒ 2/3	工 gōng 2/3								
38.	氵 shuǐ water	没 méi 1/17	法 fǎ 1/21	汽 qì 1/43	海 hǎi 1/49	湾 wān 1/49	洲 zhōu 2/1	洗 xǐ 2/5	浴 yù 2/6	活 huó 2/9	江 jiāng 2/9
		河 hé 2/9	湖 hú 2/9	游 yóu 2/13	泳 yǒng 2/13						
39.	宀 mián roof	字 zì 1/8	家 jiā 1/18	容 róng 1/28	客 kè 2/5	室 shì 2/5	寒 hán 2/11	宫 gōng 2/12	完 wán 2/16	寄 jì 2/18	
40.	门 mén door	间 jiān 2/3	门 mén 2/3	闹 nào 2/4							

	Radical	**Characters**									
41.	辶 chuò stop & go	这 zhè 1/12	还 hái 1/20	远 yuǎn 1/48	近 jìn 1/48	边 biān 2/1	过 guò 2/1	送 sòng 2/2	道 dào 2/6	进 jìn 2/8	运 yùn 2/13
		连 lián 2/13	迟 chí 2/15								
42.	忄 xīn heart	快 kuài 1/30	怕 pà 2/7	忙 máng 2/10	恭 gōng 2/10	懂 dǒng 2/14	惯 guàn 2/16	愉 yú 2/18			
43.	廾 gǒng cup hands	开 kāi 2/3									
44.	大 dà big	大 dà 1/6	太 tài 1/10	天 tiān 1/31							
45.	广 yǎn cliff	店 diàn 2/2	度 dù 2/11	应 yīng 2/11							
46.	夕 xī evening	多 duō 1/24	岁 suì 1/37	外 wài 2/4							
47.	寸 cùn tiny	封 fēng 2/4	对 duì 2/14								
48.	己 jǐ self	已 yǐ 2/4									
49.	小 xiǎo small	小 xiǎo 1/1	少 shǎo 1/24								
50.	夊 suī slow walk	夏 xià 2/8	冬 dōng 2/8								
51.	饣 shí eat	饭 fàn 1/40	馆 guǎn 1/42	饿 è 2/15							

	Radical	**Characters**									
52.	犭 quǎn dog	狗 gǒu 1/36	猫 māo 1/37								
53.	子 zǐ son	学 xué 1/9	孩 hái 1/25	子 zǐ 1/25							
54.	弓 gōng bow	张 zhāng 1/24									
55.	尢 wāng cripple	就 jiù 2/6									
56.	扌 shǒu hand	把 bǎ 2/10	打 dǎ 2/11	拍 pāi 2/12	找 zhǎo 2/13	换 huàn 2/15	报 bào 2/16				
57.	方 fāng square	方 fāng 2/1	旅 lǚ 2/12								
58.	歹 dǎi bad	死 sǐ 2/15									
59.	父 fù father	爸 bà 1/16									
60.	文 wén writing	文 wén 1/1									
61.	日 rì sun	日 rì 1/2	是 shì 1/3	易 yì 1/28	明 míng 1/32	昨 zuó 1/32	星 xīng 1/33	早 zǎo 1/40	晚 wǎn 1/40	时 shí 2/6	晴 qíng 2/7
		春 chūn 2/8	暑 shǔ 2/11								
62.	曰 yuē speak	最 zuì 1/20									

	Radical	Characters
63.	月 yuè moon	月 yuè 1/2 朋 péng 1/9 有 yǒu 1/17 期 qī 1/33 服 fú 2/10 望 wàng 2/11 脑 nǎo 2/13
64.	木 mù wood	校 xiào 1/15 本 běn 1/23 枝 zhī 1/23 椅 yǐ 2/5 桌 zhuō 2/5 楼 lóu 2/5 样 yàng 2/7 树 shù 2/8 机 jī 2/9 架 jià 2/17
65.	灬 huǒ fire	点 diǎn 1/50 然 rán 2/5 热 rè 2/7 照 zhào 2/12
66.	火 huǒ fire	火 huǒ 1/43
67.	心 xīn heart	您 nín 1/6 想 xiǎng 1/26 念 niàn 1/35 怎 zěn 2/3 忘 wàng 2/16 急 jí 2/17 感 gǎn 2/18
68.	手 shǒu hand	手 shǒu 2/5 拿 ná 2/10
69.	爪 zhǎo claws	爱 ài 1/19
70.	斤 jīn ax	新 xīn 1/12
71.	欠 qiàn owe	歌 gē 1/27 欢 huān 1/30
72.	王 wáng king	王 wáng 1/2 玩 wán 1/22 班 bān 2/4 现 xiàn 2/12 理 lǐ 2/14
73.	户 hù door	所 suǒ 1/39 房 fáng 2/5
74.	礻 shì show	礼 lǐ 2/12 祝 zhù 2/18

	Radical	Characters				
75.	戈 gē spear	我 wǒ 1/3	或 huò 2/6	成 chéng 2/16		
76.	牛 niú ox	牛 niú 1/36	物 wù 2/12	特 tè 2/17		
77.	毛 máo hair	毛 máo 1/25				
78.	毋 wú do not	每 měi 1/50				
79.	穴 xué cave	穿 chuān 2/10	空 kōng 2/18			
80.	衤 yī clothes	初 chū 1/35	裤 kù 1/45	被 bèi 2/17		
81.	片 piàn piece	片 piàn 2/12				
82.	气 qì air	气 qì 2/7				
83.	攵 pū tap	教 jiāo 1/26	放 fàng 2/10	故 gù 2/12	数 shǔ 2/14	收 shōu 2/18
84.	水 shuǐ water	水 shuǐ 1/29				
85.	钅 jīn metal	钱 qián 1/38	银 yín 2/2	钟 zhōng 2/15		
86.	田 tián field	男 nán 1/11	电 diàn 1/13	界 jiè 2/1		

	Radical	**Characters**						
87.	白 bái white	的 de 1/8	百 bǎi 1/38	白 bái 1/44				
88.	西 xī west	要 yào 1/26	西 xī 1/47					
89.	目 mù eye	看 kàn 1/26						
90.	比 bǐ compare	比 bǐ 1/20						
91.	疒 chuáng illness	病 bìng 2/15						
92.	矢 shǐ arrow	知 zhī 2/6						
93.	禾 hé grains	秋 qiū 2/8	科 kē 2/14					
94.	用 yòng use	用 yòng 1/22						
95.	竹 zhú bamboo	笔 bǐ 1/23	筷 kuài 1/42	第 dì 2/1	等 děng 2/6	笑 xiào 2/7	算 suàn 2/11	箱 xiāng 2/17
96.	老 lǎo old	老 lǎo 1/10	者 zhě 2/6	考 kǎo 2/16				
97.	羊 yáng sheep	美 měi 1/4	羊 yáng 1/36					
98.	臣 chén minister	卧 wò 2/6						

	Radical	Characters
99.	虍 hū tiger	虎 hǔ 1/35
100.	衣 yī clothes	衣 yī 1/45 表 biǎo 2/15
101.	舟 zhōu boat	船 chuán 2/9 航 háng 2/18
102.	贝 bèi shell	贵 guì 1/7
103.	见 jiàn see	觉 jué 2/4 见 jiàn 2/6
104.	走 zǒu walk	起 qǐ 2/2 走 zǒu 2/3 越 yuè 2/8 趣 qù 2/14
105.	车 chē cart	车 chē 1/43 辆 liàng 1/43
106.	里 lǐ neighborhood	里 lǐ 2/4
107.	隹 zhuī bird	难 nán 1/28 雄 xióng 2/17
108.	金 jīn metal	金 jīn 1/38
109.	雨 yǔ rain	零 líng 1/14 雨 yǔ 2/7 雪 xuě 2/7 雷 léi 2/7
110.	食 shí eat	食 shí 2/2 餐 cān 2/9

	Radical	**Characters**
111.	风 fēng wind	风 fēng 2/9
112.	音 yīn sound	音 yīn 2/15
113.	革 gé rawhide	鞋 xié 1/45
114.	页 yè page	题 tí 2/16
115.	马 mǎ horse	马 mǎ 1/6
116.	鸟 niǎo bird	鸟 niǎo 1/29
117.	黑 hēi black	黑 hēi 1/44
118.	龙 lóng dragon	龙 lóng 1/35